Rotate 90 degrees clockwise
[FOR BEST READABILITY]

THE *New* LAYMAN'S ALMANAC

Poems by

JACOB McARTHUR MOONEY

McClelland & Stewart

LIBRARY AND ARCHIVES CANADA CATALOGUING IN PUBLICATION

Mooney, Jacob McArthur
The new layman's almanac : poems / Jacob McArthur Mooney.

ISBN 978-0-7710-5407-5

I. Title.

PS8626.O5928N49 2008   C811'.6   C2007-907403-0

We acknowledge the financial support of the Government of Canada through the Book Publishing Industry Development Program and that of the Government of Ontario through the Ontario Media Development Corporation's Ontario Book Initiative. We further acknowledge the support of the Canada Council for the Arts and the Ontario Arts Council for our publishing program.

Typeset in Granjon by M&S, Toronto
Printed and bound in Canada

This book is printed on acid-free paper that is 100% recycled, ancient-forest friendly (100% post-consumer recycled).

McClelland & Stewart Ltd.
75 Sherbourne Street
Toronto, Ontario
M5A 2P9
www.mcclelland.com

1   2   3   4   5   12   11   10   09   08

"I have a video vision of infinitely exhilarating pluralism."

— **LESTER BANGS**

NO. 1   *A Guide to* Locomotion

NO. 2   *A Guide to* Reversing

NO. 3   *A Guide to* Immortality

NO. 4   *A Guide to* Drinking in the Rain

NO. 5   *A Guide to* Disempowerment

NO. 6   *A Guide to* Enjambment

NO. 7   *A Guide to* Newfoundland

NO. 8   *A Guide to* Going in Easy

NO. 9   *A Guide to* the Physical Development of the Storm

NO. 10   *A Guide to* Syncopation

NO. 11   *A Guide to* Impermanency

NO. 12   *A Guide to* Breaking the Banking Industry

NO. 13   *A Guide to* Rural Routes

NO. 14   *A Guide to* Refraction

NO. 15   *A Guide to* Remaining Skeptical of Your Power as a Voter

NO. 16   *A Guide to* Alternate Histories

NO. 17   *A Guide for* Writers Dying of Alcoholism

NO. 18   *A Guide to* the House at 6 Arthur Hatt Road

NO. 19 A *Guide to* the Application of H_2O_2

NO. 20 A *Guide to* Sabermetrics

NO. 21 A *Guide to* Punishment

NO. 22 A *Guide to* Leftovers

NO. 23 A *Guide to* Exhibition

NO. 24 A *Guide to* Life Cycles

NO. 25 A *Guide to* the Visual Arts

NO. 26 A *Guide to* Chord Progression

NO. 27 A *Guide to* the Erasure of Spandau Prison

NO. 28 A *Guide to* the Material Record

NO. 29 A *Guide to* Getting It Wrong

NO. 30 A *Guide to* the Death of Dr. Haing S. Ngor

NO. 31 A *Guide to* Conscientiousness

NO. 32 A *Guide to* Getting It Right

APPENDIX A: Various World: The Pinsky Variations

APPENDIX B: Contrast Negotiations, '05–'07

Postscripture

THE *New* LAYMAN'S ALMANAC

Poems

A Guide to LOCOMOTION

(SEE ALSO: *"night blindness"*; *"perceived stress as a variable in experimental design"*)

Here's something –

I'm awake at four a.m. and the lights are off in the house, this
lets me see outside, but stops outside from seeing in.

There's a man lumping down Oxen Pond Road, off Freshwater, no bending
at the knees. Everything the walk is about comes to this: heel-shift-

toe-shift. The man is bleeding
from his head, his hands, chest.

Each of the three light poles between the corner and my driveway
add depth. What colour is blood? Ask the oxygen. Breathe.

Then there's this –

The man doesn't stop at the 24-hour bakery.
He loses his balance

on a dry patch of pavement, shucks over into my neighbour's hibernating
rose bush. There's a moan, somewhere. His fixed jaws hold firm.

The man drips – clumped gushes of giving. For the roses, fresh blooms.
Summer flinches in its sleep. Here, have this. I-love-you-so-forget-me-not. A cat

halves the road, breaches the borderland of light from the poles. In certain spots,
there's ice – in others, nothing. The surface goes unblinking. Black

and friction-dimpled. The forced erosion of cars and trucks and things that
push. Eaten asphalt. My favourite animal is the earthworm. Grip. Reach. Drag.

A front-wheel drive car is essentially a tow truck. The back tires spin because it's
easier than stopping. I get it. The man is running fingers through his hair.

He gets up,

offers for the first time an agreement with his legs, spits defiance at the ground, in direction of the frozen cat. One big lucky step and his momentum keeps him

moving. As he passes my window, I flick the light switch. Surprise. You win. I call after him, *Are you alright, buddy?* In one swing he turns, bends low to

the ground and grabs a stone, side-arms it at my window. Misses, gen-

erously. And then he's running. I am drinking decaf coffee. The cat is running – paws catch the ground and then release it (carnivorewargames). This happened in January

in the city's East End. If you'll follow the presumption, I wasn't even holding that coffee mug, I was teaching it to stand.

A Guide to REVERSING

(SEE ALSO: *"internal combustion"; "measuring loss due to entropy in an open system"*)

Subvocal. The message is quivered
like a mumble down a tuning wand:

axle, wheel, the shadow of the wheel,
spinning. A groan-soft pain in your foot,

or (say-it-with-me) *your sole.* Who has
heard regret? Not the word but the inflec-

tion it presents, the sound of a
parenthesis: closed, then reopened . . . .

A Guide to IMMORTALITY

(SEE ALSO: "cancers: theatrical"; "National Parks of Canada"; "aquatic safety"; "1988")

The rising action of our
adolescent argument:

My dog's fast.

Mine's faster.

Fastest.

    Let's just stand back to
back and see which one of us
                is taller.

=

Across the park your sister sits
      high in the backwood

weeds like this is Definitely the summer she reads *Catcher in*
the Rye and kisses a local
with hair longer

      than hers is.

||

Five mermaids line the dock
        down the hill, while
four older boys, on hands and knees,
               look

down into
      their humid eyes,
      their catalogue
      one-pieces.

||

Kids dressed as adults and
kids dressed as soldiers and
their fathers dressed as retiring
NFL quarterbacks – the day thickening
to a syrup, the heat a limp
body,   the sun as a reflection of my face in
your soda.

||

                In eight weeks
it'll be fall again, the province considering
who to hire out for
snow removal in the park.   In six weeks
                            the schools will open, in six years your
                            your family moved out to the
                            West Coast, you the quiet
                            Maritimer with the hair like
sister will have drowned,

seaweed in your face. Both arms folded on the school bus in
Vancouver,
                        Weezer on the headphones, staring
        accusations at
        the folds of
        another ocean.

The rhythm of
its waves mimic
the falsetto of

Eastern songbirds, or
the pattern of the lift chairs

in Whistler.

A Guide to DRINKING IN THE RAIN

(SEE ALSO: "*disrepair*"; "*a certain lack of moral courage*"; "*the exhibitionists at nightfall*")

What's this called? *A meniscus. A hundred instant
strip-mines, testing at my skin.* Experience

erosion. What's this called? *Grounded.
The only difference between lying down*

and flying. In six months they'll pile snow
on the grass, spring will come and it'll still

be there, confusing baby jaybirds. Foreboding, for
animals that don't think. Foreshadowing is a

product of belief. Six more months and we'd
be frozen to the ground, but tomorrow,

kids will come here and play soccer. Their
mums will find my beer bottles. Yours, too.

There will be a shaking of heads. There'll be
much discussion on the strength

of our community, the sanctity
of gates.

A Guide to DISEMPOWERMENT

(SEE ALSO: *"welfare policies of the good years"; "the civilian complex"; "love"*)

A woman in this building

lived with her two

young kids on the federal cheques. She cleaned houses to

buy extras, one of her

clients was the wife of a local

government official. When the guy found out, he put a call in

to his boss. The lady lost

the welfare, then

her car, then

the kids. A sad sad

story. Unsure who

to dedicate the poem to. Skinny kids can't eat

ink and paper, the client's husband

never told her what happened, they vowed to keep work

and family life

separate. The only thing left
                    (well, in fact there's
nothing left, but a moralist hangs his
hat on what's around)
          is the
government official. Everything is dedicated
to his valued honesty, his sense of
good works, the institution that granted
his professional degree
          (... his bedroom community, Jean-Jacques
Rousseau, the founders of the nation ...)

A Guide to ENJAMBMENT

(SEE ALSO: *"chainsaw sculptures"*; *"jazz delivery"*; *"ch-ch-check"*)

I

woke up and the girls who

lived across the street were

pretending to be cowboys. They had

two sticks with horse heads affixed to

the ends, they were galloping down

the one-lane laughing, experts at improbably mapping

a four-legged system's

gait

in bipedal half-time. I

heard of drummers that can work

like that, one arm banging out two-four and the other, three-eight on the same kit. It's

easy to see how

the act of expression

grows

from an awkward
stutter-
step, the point where
chaos becomes
chance, becomes
order, becomes
time.

A Guide to NEWFOUNDLAND

(SEE ALSO: "St. John's Harbour, from the corner of Prescott and Water. Fall, maybe eight a.m.")

This is the haven where the haunting
hits you first. The gulls float home, balanced

on their wings, like ash folded back
into earth, flakes lost from a fire on The Hill.

The harbour
wraps out like two

scarred arms, greedy, hoping for another
small claim to the land. It ends here. The whole
world.

This island did not go down
agreeing. A limping workhorse charges

on first sight of the farmer's rifle. Our ride
kicked twice, leaving matching bumps

on the grass, grey pockets of bruising, before
she gave out, went limp, and died. The narrows

defeat her, all the passing icebergs
stand
to see her effigies,
	engraved.

A Guide to GOING IN EASY *(for W.)*

(SEE ALSO: *"negotiation in domestic disturbances"; "archetypal male failure-rates"*)

There's too little
Sunday left
to be this greedy with
your time. You ate those words
out of boredom, not
because you were hungry. A distrust of language, and it's

showing in your cheeks.

Another story about the
whorehouses in Edmonton. Fort Saskatchewan: McMurray: fortresses. Did I hear this one?

I once left a pay cheque uncashed for fifteen weeks, you say.

Those girls, you say,
all they knew was how to
get in out of the rain.

We eat. Out of boredom. *Never had*
so much nothing as today. Shouldn't have said those things
to the ex.   *– I know.*

I see it. In your eyes: magnetism. Poles from:

New-   Costa

foundland   to   Rica.   Retirement. Umbrella drinks.

                                The balsa wood of living.

     How about it,

those hard boys at the work camps?

                                (Transfer payments: transplants: transgression)

         – They left their grumble
         in the bottom of your voice,
         like the tar lining your lungs from
         those cigarettes you don't
         smoke.

Yellow on
my walls. Damage deposit: bad mornings: mourning. My voices

jam
in accidental complication.

Going halfs on another half case. A mean denial of every last charge. Yes, I'll come to the
station in the morning. Yes, I'm a good friend. No,
I didn't drink the Budweiser. I
don't drink Budweiser.

Epilogue:
There's a switchblade knife on the fireplace. Fuckers
would take it off me, never give it back if
they could. Have it. All my problems
are drinking problems . . . something
about drowning . . . sniffle . . . yawn.

Hands in: face: in hands. Head in hands. Hands in

armpits in the car. Freezing. Both windows open to air the
bastard out.   *Cold is a kind of nothing.   – Is it?*

Leaving, a constable asks me
my relation to the man. I turn and walk out
of the station. Nobody stops me. *Nobody stop me!* In the daybreak,

street signs: faded:
everything going on chance.

A Guide to THE PHYSICAL DEVELOPMENT OF THE STORM

(SEE ALSO: "temperance"; "September"; "barometric pressure"; page 130)

i. I know, Dad, how the hurricane is shaped.

You and the storm share a
sudden lucid downbeat. Eyes.
The house   stops shaking and
        you lean over your
                cigarette-fog,
                say *Do you   want to see it,*
                        the weather?

ii. This is the year before you left. The rain is hot above us.

We don alert-coloured coats, tuck jeans into
        boots, heads into caps. We stand like

rookie centurions before the filtered sheet of water
running from the roof,   and our reflections are
            darker, cleaner in its
                warped,
                bevelled glass.

You stick a hand out,
your old   tumbler filling to
completion in seconds.

You smile, say, *Cheers!* and then
                duck
                into

the patient black light.   This small gift
from the wind-gods to the storm's worst hit.
                The eye.

iii. My sister's bicycle around us;

    horn,

        basket, then

                the bike itself, like

the victim of a fall from heights, its

    legs bent out   to either side and the frame

        split open, like it was pressed too tight

                  to hold

                    the pipe.

iv. The storm has a borrowed foreign name.

        Exotic. Can you imagine all

this well-travelled thing has seen? The eyes? Can you smell

her air, which is not like our air,   our pickled,

salty, drunk-on-the-ocean, too fat and lazy

            to go anywhere air?

v. I see you dancing in the backyard and my socks are getting wet.

Would this have happened if you weren't such
    a drinker? Do other fathers
do this?   Would they channel fake
scientific know-how, adopt a
    professorial tone, the mud chasing
      down your cheeks like
      matching,   masculine,
        mud-stained tears?

vi. The wind kicks up, you adapt with, *This isn't really*

    the eye, you see. The Cubans would call it
    "The Blight," or   *"The Short Breath" because*
    there was only time to suck back a single
      quick smoke.   A tree branch screams
      past my head, the rain shifts sideways:
        a-million-battle-movie-arrows. You cup

a mouth organ from the den of your pocket
and I make out my mother,
quiet,   in the kitchen yellow.
and Mom made you promise
if it started getting worse, you'd hurry me back home. She made sure to
make you swear.

A zoo tiger sees everything,

vii. The blowing hardens, bloats into a constancy of wind,

rain, and sound. I press my hands against it, remove
gloves and feel the world huffing down in shouts
from on above us.   All these lucky beads of wander
go crystal at my palms.

viii. Dad, I understand now you were calling it a *Jew's Harp*,

that convex twanging echo from your teeth. It's only been
these last few years I've realized it's not *Juice Harp* or
Jew Sharp.   I don't want to find you

reading this and worry

I'm making public some

concealed backhand wart, it's not

your fault, it's   and

                your father's,   and

          his father's,

ix. I turn to step out of your slipstream completely.

You look up, across the hill to our neighbours'
          upturned lawn.   *We should head in*

soon, you say and neither of us moves. The whole
animal earth claws itself around us,   screaming loose
          a hole sound enough that we could both step through it.

                                        An eye.

x. The wind collapses, exhausted at your lips. A smile sits upon them:

victorious, hard. The gust gives out and
I step forward towards you to keep myself
from falling.   The light from the house flashes at
your zipper, I lean in and press my forehead to your chest.

Our breath and   heartbeats bop
syncopated through
our ears, echoed in the
hollows   that are home to
our eyes.

xi. The sky sticks a hand out to hold up its architecture.

The stars wink on above us,
from a distance
so dangerous,
it hasn't yet
been mapped.

A Guide to SYNCOPATION

(SEE ALSO DON MCKAY'S "BONE POEMS": *Holy Cow. Some creature*
so completely music that its bones

burst into song.
Now we understand those stories of the savage

pianist, annually growing hands . . .")

Up like a pre-
addict Jerry Lee Lewis

at four-thirty in the morning. Did you know I once
took lessons? Chop, chop-hands ranging down, a chorus of

small bells. Did you know I never even
had to practise? Higher, higher, fourthing up the octaves. Damn this

stubborn anchor. Miller, more wood! Kill me an elephant, we need
more keys in here! Get another stool, my arm's

too short to reach the end. An endangered species, bloodied up
outside, and me with my machine, wowing up a stretch to leap the Atlantic, swing

out across the mountains of Old Europe. Mozart: Beethoven: Marconi. If we
built a piano that wrapped around the world, inventing higher notes, piercing glass, killing

small dogs, knocking the moon from its orbit —
and it returned to its domestic roots
in snowy Eastern Canada, what would we call its point of contact with the original
bass beginning?

What would we call that note?

A Guide to **IMPERMANENCY**

(SEE ALSO: *"fiat money"; "a numerologist's grasp of advanced calculus"; page 123*)

The businessman's jacket is too hot
for this weather. He tries again,
the machine first accepts his
dollar bill, then reneges and
pushes it away, the left corner is torn and the
circuits will not read it.

This problem is common among articles of faith.

The man gives up, turns to walk away.
After three profanities he stops: What if
he had a bigger bill with a tear
in the corner? A fifty? A hundred?
A thousand? What if all his
stowed-away money in glass banks across

the world was found to be defective, machines
would not accept it?

Or with one bad pass through an airport
scanner, would his credit cards fail

a store's electric test?

A Guide to BREAKING THE BANKING INDUSTRY

(SEE ALSO: *"national fiscal policies, 1980–present"; the work of Dr. Robert Oltman*)

They only keep a fifth
of their money in the vault at a time. What it means is this:

If you can convince one-
quarter of the town to withdraw their whole accounts on

the same morning, they'll
run out. Make sure you're next in line when this happens.

Say this: *Don't have my
eighty-five dollars, eh? Well, those sure are some good*

lookin' shoes. The next guy
steps up and buys out all the cameras, which is about to

be important, because
by ten there's no cars left in the driveway. By eleven-thirty

the building's mortgaged out
to a conglomerate from Elm Street. The manager agrees to

indentured servitude with
the *Cleanliness Patrol* in the park. Present this story to

a banker at a restaurant,
when he dismisses the threat, ask him: *So who's paying*

for this cheque, me or you?

35

A Guide to RURAL ROUTES

(SEE ALSO: "Trunk 14, Nova Scotia Highway System"; "tectonics"; page 116)

Bipolar road. You could drive
the whole way on the wrong side
and not worry. Stretch, it stretches
out, empty, and then some lonely house,
with sixty feet of fencing and a guard dog.
Chopped wood and it never stops raining.
Get out of the car and feel for the midpoint,
crouch down, focus, you're the fulcrum.
Balance point for the road, the province.
Shift and one sinks away.

A Guide to REFRACTION

(SEE ALSO: *"mating practices of the North American male"; "mock transcendence"*)

Eight-thirty a.m.
in August. I know how sunlight
expresses the airplanes

through the cloudbank above
the lake. This is all I learned
about reflection, that and the prism

trick – you hold the thing up and
it threads the light out. Doctors in
TV science programs said *This is all*

there is, these seven ordered
bands, or, at least *This is all*
there seems to be. I wrote that on a

science test, went home, and cried. You and I
used to complain that way about
perception. I watch you now, through

my rain-hood-and-coffee-cup frame, skipping stones
towards the fog. I rub my eyes until you melt
down, separate into structure, your indigos and

reds lasered back to me at ten to the
something
metres a second. Your disassembled self finds

my glasses, the skin on
my forehead, all around me, this
grass, the tent-pole damaged Earth.

A Guide to REMAINING SKEPTICAL OF YOUR POWER AS A VOTER

(SEE ALSO: *"political behaviour of low-income earners"; "feeding the jaws that bite you"*)

Market Value = two men walking

down a rocky path holding a paved

road over their heads. One turns to

the other and as the concrete crumbles

around their bleeding hands, he says

The revolution is all spin, you know.

The revolution is all spin. Everything

the world wants to know about you

fits in most-used pockets of your pants.

Don't be angry or surprised. The revolution,

the revolution, the revolution is all spin. So

give me your vengeful dancing, your

daylong intellectual riffs. Give me
a taste of that hot wax, burning. Give
me the revolution, the revolution is all
spin. The revolution (devolution), the

revolution is all spin.

A Guide to ALTERNATE HISTORIES

(SEE ALSO: *"the first summer post–high school"; "poisoning the soil"*)

Take a step to the left. Take another. There
was this photograph I shrugged off once
while moving, me and the hard local girl who
taught me the words to Basket Case, bent
from the roots into each other like the letter A.
Each time I saw her she'd ask me my birthday,
sometimes even wrote it down. I don't know, maybe
she wanted to be the first person to ever record
everybody's. Her best friend shot the picture,

Take a step to the left. Take another. There,
I got it. They both died in a car wreck, hit a ten-seat
van in their rental, pieces of vacation thrown around
an acre of New Brunswick like late-night unloading
beside a tight-made bed in the next motel down the list.
Thanks for coming. I asked her what she wanted once

we graduated, she said first whatever, then college. I said first college, then whatever and no I can't go with you. She said whatever. *(S)he said my life's a bore.*

They found her in a cornfield, fingers clawed into the soil, as if she spent her last seconds praying for return. Her name was Martha but I often misspeak and call her Martyr. *Sometimes I give myself the creeps. Sometimes my mind plays tricks on me.* The farmer went and sold his land, moved in with his brother in Moncton. You'll pass the place if you're driving to Quebec, get out at the first exit you don't recognize, walk into the parking lot. Take a step to the left. Take another,

there.

A Guide for WRITERS DYING OF ALCOHOLISM

(SEE THE BOOK: Answered Prayers: The Unfinished Novel *by Truman Capote*)

First, do no harm, there are
    things you could say that might. Focus

to a point of such refusal
    that your breath becomes self-reference.

There are exercises. Also, there's
    hotels with doors that lock from the inside.

Act out in public, but privately,
    act in. And bushel your books together like a

habit in your bedroom. No one
    wants to be outspoken, it causes a strain in

the voice. Okay, you're drowning,
   but talking just fills the lungs faster. Friends say

you're entirely too wrong in
   your living. Say this: *To be entirely anything*

is a sign of some progression
   for a complication such as us. I won't pretend

to be feeding you these lines, these
   prayers, unanswered by a God that's in the decals.

You define a week's consumption
   biblically: a jeroboam, a nebuchadnezzar, a

melchiar (to the punt). What's
   impressive is how you can taste it back

to the scenic happenstance
    of grapes, how you perceive in things

their nurseries, or the seeds
    held unstudied in the skin of domestic trees.

A Guide to THE HOUSE AT 6 ARTHUR HATT ROAD

(SEE ALSO: *"popular histories"*; *"The Winfrey Doctrine"*; *"lies about the neighbours"*)

The house was built to face, bravely,
the far edges of the world. That kitchen
had doors like estuaries, five
of them in all. The following
is a recent history of their contents
— edited for entertainment.

The 1st door faced the sun
and as such
gets recalled in fuzzy yellows, blurred
by squint vision. It led
to a pantry, and then
the basement stairs
— rubber boots and flashlights piled
in the corner. Everything

breathed, and was haunted
by field mice. Newspapers announced the 1940s.
Your daughter's cat would sleep on the deep freeze,
having snuck in the prey way.
Bloated and content,
it would think up ways to kill me in my sleep.
There's your well-fed protector
that I never trusted. Don't trust animals
that mock their meals. I could tell
it was evil, that it held careful secrets – when I was
four months old, the thing slept on my face and
I broke out like dandelions
on the May two-four weekend.

The 2nd door led outside,
through it our neighbour came on Christmas Eves,
decked in red and white.
Starting in 1987,
he would show up every year

all whisky and festive, floppy cheer.
His elfin wife, four-foot-eight
would often sleep all week,
but on her good days she'd
gladly throw assorted balls
across our broken fence with me, and
explore the foundations of dead houses
in the woods behind the kitchen door.
She once had schoolteacher ambitions,
but settled on being a headcase.
Settling again,
she died in October, 1993.
She ate crushed pills for the brain-sick and
stage-dove off her headboard

— I was given the details four years later.
We had the wake in the kitchen,
and that night, removed neckties, you
peeling off your pointed shoes, us

switching to the den to watch the World Series.
The fear of God not diluted
by unending sleep-filled Sundays,
we left the kitchen doors open
so that He would feel welcome.

The 3rd door opened
onto a psychotropic purple carpet and a room
the realtor called a *half bath*
   – the mirror was six inches wide.
I held the door shut
through the Mulroney administration,
and half the Chrétien years
for the girl next door
   – archetypal and actual.
She coddled lonely like a runty newborn
puppy, grew an ulcer by grade five,
and dangled transcendence
from a fish hook,
five inches in front of her face.

I remember cupcakes in the kitchen,
the smell of flour and lip gloss,
the taste of brown sugar,
and

most importantly,
learning how to lie to old people.
Somewhere in the sunburns, our heads
grew small like cameras. Beautiful
and bored, we found ourselves,
swollen to the flood lines
by 1996.

The 4th door spilled onto the dining room
(where empires fell).
I saw you, broken in the doorframe.
The paint was chipped, our
night of lost knives
    — and it was never fixed
        just beautifully ignored.

I stepped over broken dishes to get at paper plates.
I wondered whether to ask you for the milk.
That was 1998,
when the plane fell from the sky
as I studied world capitals
at the kitchen table. I swear
I saw its lights flicker
and felt the window's heartbeat as the sound wave passed (*whadoomp*).
On December 31st we stayed in and subvocalized
on the hard slow death of the year, you with your
wine which came in boxes, and me
in new Christmas clothing,
protected from the sideways snowstorm. Speechless, we
listened to the gun club
shooting off across the street.

The 5th door was a mystery
solved as we stayed in
painting over bite marks

in June, 1999.

Behind the oven and the spice rack,
covered by layered paper, it
silently outlasted us.

It opened, to three inches of empty space
and a note. We held back
a collective

How'd we miss this? Now,
these houses have their secrets,
locked away, wedged between boards, where
our greedy new-mentia can't find them.

Witnesses to everything,
social scientists,
that house lived
in the squeaks and creaks and whistles
it shared with us

     – a willing participant, an equal.

A piece of paper, yellow-old,
hung by a nail at shoulder-height.

Holding it up,
we folded our eyes,
its marks not seen since the day it was new.
It read:

"Art built this:
"April 1st, 1902."

A Guide to THE APPLICATION OF H$_2$O$_2$

(SEE ALSO: *"proper maintenance of one's toenails"; "a jackknife and crossed fingers"*)

Goodbye,   mysticisms.   We knew it
would end like this. Goodbye, physical integrity
of my toe. I was told if I ignored it, there'd be a
        chance of   infection.

Molarity.   Argentum.   Plumbum.
What more would I know if I had learned Latin?
If I hadn't walked out on science, I'd be
one hell of a well-read pharmacist. Look here –
the nail bed: rabid, expansive. I'm becoming the
        air near   my feet.

Revive   dramatic   medicines!
My ancestors' TB bull's eyes (an illness that knew
where it stood) or the hard intolerance of an
iron lung. Call me phlegmatic, but whatever
        became   of leprosy?

Splash,   pause,   grumble,

and hiss. Was there anything so graceful as the
death of the wicked witch? The peroxide divides
into exponents of rocket fuel. How this is safe,
I'm not sure. Control is evidenced by the fact

    I'm not   melting.

Pus.   Poison.   Possibility.
Is there anything you can still get for which
they'll give you leeches? Maybe we're
revolted by parasites because they sur-
vive by realigning the lines that separate

      the alive   from

every-   thing   else.
The happy chaos of my infinite end
reinterprets cleansing through dance.
The pain must be somewhere in the
bubbles; it's gone. Either amputated
from me,   or me from it.

A Guide to SABERMETRICS

(SEE THE FOLLOWING: *Sabermetrics: (n) Baseball term, a method of algorithmically determining the size of an individual player's contribution to his team. Also the name of the strategies employed by its proponents (most notably by Oakland Athletics General Manager Billy Beane). Invented by Bill James and the Society for American Baseball Research (SABR).*)

Officially the field didn't end, not until they went

and put a fence out there to stop it. They wanted to
add seats in the back and sell tickets. Blame Babe Ruth

and a surge in post-war attendance. Blame the
live ball movement and the ways of market
capitalism. Blame Billy Beane. Blame the Green

Monster, once you give a nickname to your pen,
the butcher can't be asked to think in terms of sacrifice.
And so what if a triangle's just three separate ambitions
that capped each other's stretch? I know these things

about Stockholm: the syndrome, the Peace Prize,
and Marcus, who only ever watched golf and
the triathlon, wouldn't allow for enclosures on
the race to human excellence. He hated the arrogance
in how I said *a perfect game*. I called him an idealist,

then winced as the bad guys hit a one hopper past
the ads. Ground rule. So blame Billy Beane, blame
Bill James and Giambi and Mark Mulder. Blame
the finite backs of baseball cards. Blame me,
I once knew the RBI leaders
on every Major League team. That one sure was

    a year worth
    insisting occurred.

A Guide to PUNISHMENT

(SEE ALSO: *"the collected autobiographies of J. and J. Doe"; "mftbgjmh ojuf"*)

Alright. So now here's one for the martyrs among us. Everybody
in this bit wears a uniform, *sowatchout.*

You pay for attention with your tax dollars, citizens, the whole value of revenge
is the first three seconds post-impact. If you miss it there's no encore.
They can build it up with better lighting, or a strong performance
from the vanquished.

What we need is to be told that we're disgusting. What we get is a reminder
of the bluntness of our organs, their tendency to leak when attacked.

Moses took dictation to the best of his talents, but it's hard to write on rock and
he missed the amendment about the rules
only counting once per head. It's okay if the names run together
or are hard to pronounce, faces are either covered or
strapped-back so The Gallery can't see them.

If I knew an elected official, I'd recommend that
the families
be seated in a shared room. If the point is to transplant suffering, imagine
how looking into the son-of-a-bitch's mother's eyes would
add value to the acquisition. There's votes there for an innovator.

Saying it doesn't happen in Canada's like saying it never happened to you.
Any argument based on statistics just
paints the room a darker red. Squint and you could
lose it in the darkness, mistake it
for blood on the walls.

A Guide to LEFTOVERS

(SEE ALSO: *"dietary habits of high-school seniors vs. dietary habits of college freshmen"*)

The easiest is pizza, in
forty concentrated seconds it's
just as good as the day it was
ordered.

But if you need to start mixing
separate frozen elements, it gets
progressively tougher. The right hand
starts reaching for the
precooked ham
                and mayo. The worst is
spaghetti sauce, for eighteen years
I unearthed forgotten tubs from the
guts of my

mother's freezer, each advertising

Chocolate or *Mocha Fudge*, I would

wash my favourite novelty spoon,

find the scooper in the pantry, then

peel back the

top to find a mess of crystal

monkey brains. I still can't look at

red stains on a white lid without

fighting back

the need to

gag myself in protest.

A Guide to EXHIBITION

(SEE THE BOOK: *John de Visser's* Historic Newfoundland; "*The Rooms Art Gallery, St. John's*")

Glass is sex by open invitation, a voluntary invasion
and you martyr yourself off for
art, science, pageantry. Observations.

Six rivers of light frame the atrium, the worker's named the rays
after her favourite photographers.
She felt they needed something less general than *sun*.

A man with a Dutch name shipped down with a camera,
and a steamer loaded full of
outsider eyes so bold they popped the skin tectonic.

Make a point to shoot for your readership. They need to
see in these themselves, or else
see photography for the fiat currency it is. Borders

are a set of circular arguments, the worshipping
of walls. National. Geographic. *So too
is glass.* A young man from the mainland stands

in a room full of picture frames, back turned
to the panorama that
shows off the city like a beaming ethno-entomologist.

The fog bends to the lens, smokes through the walls and
shows up in the pictures. The girl in the last one
smiles past her context. How old is she today if she was twenty at the time?

Her hair falls
all the way down her neck,
shoulders, ass, floor,
the island, the planet, one second, days.

A Guide to LIFE CYCLES

(SEE ALSO: *"physical geography of the Annapolis Valley"; "church calendars"*)

i.

This is our postcard season.
I go down to the dikes
with a scalpel, and
slice off a simple red:
browning, inexpensive.

ii.

The ocean severs,
cuts blue across the province,
folds itself up and
beaches on the rocks
between the Basin and
the Bay.
     The inlets fill
with freezing, open

for the pack-ice like
wind-chilled February basements,
stretched and ready for
the leak.

iii.   Spring:

as the absence of spring. Calendar pictorials
with no hint or hue of truth. Spring consists
of fifty frozen mornings, then
falls and skins its knee, the blood
pooling into

iv.   fish season. The
bilinguals call it *summer*, and
also, *somme de mer*. Fish like
afterthoughts, sneaking through
the farsightedness of forests. Fish stuck

on the rocks, in the back of
your throat like
a toothpick,
        brittle, sharp, unrepentant, wet.

A Guide to THE VISUAL ARTS

(SEE ALSO: *"counter-programming"; "interior design"; "metaphor in public life"*)

The war
annexes
its cautious prehistory, clouds like a drop of
milk in the NY sky. Powell gets up
in front of the UN to not apologize, has
Picasso's *Guernica* covered up on
the backwall behind him. It's 2003. Begin.

(Curtain)   (Curtain)

    A peek of
      baby skin,
      a shadow on
        the shadow of
        the lamplady.

— Mr. Powell, did you order that painting covered?
   — Yes. But I didn't cover the painting.
— So did you order the painting covered?
   — Yes, but I didn't paint the thing.

Minotaur;   Minotaur;   Minotaur.
A man in a well-matched suit, tight wink
to his smile. The emptied
fallen hero of the end-of-history era. The borders of a man
                            so blurred from reshaping
                                  that to see them is to
                                     blink into astigmatism.

Someone claims they covered it
to keep away the glare, so cameras could tell
light from dark. Maybe they meant the
veteran terrors on the canvas
would white themselves away, refusing to

show up in the negatives,
like some fantastic childhood
ghost in the night, like
art in a bureaucrats' building.

A Guide to CHORD PROGRESSION

(SEE ALSO: "*Airport and Rexdale Roads, Mississauga*"; "*infestation*"; "*GTA transit overlaps*")

They imagine themselves unkillable, and free
now that they've had a fall litter. Their numbers
get them moving, run their rhythm through the house.
These mice are ancient. They see patterns that we don't.

Now that they've had a fall litter, their numbers
dream in maximums, hold on to the topmost rung until the freeze hits.
These mice are ancient. They see patterns that we don't.
Nothing I could say about survival would impress them.

Dream in maximums. Hold on to the topmost rung until the freeze hits –
someone will be hiring. They'll need you to plow snow, break ice.
Nothing I could say about survival would impress you.
You make soup on a gas stove that will last for six days.

Someone will be hiring, they'll need you to plow snow, break ice,
this city with no centre needs strong hands to unbind it.
You make soup on a gas stove that will last for six days,
invite me in to watch establishment stars in genre pictures.

This city with no centre needs strong hands to unbind it,
yours have rested on country ballads designed to numb poverty.
Invite me in. We'll watch establishment stars in genre pictures,
make music and watch the cold go by. My voice is rough, unpractised,

yours has rested on country ballads designed to numb poverty.
We develop blues lyrics about the plight of the house mouse,
make music to watch the cold go by. My voice is rough. I practise
busting the cap off a beer with the table, I fail.

We develop blues lyrics about the plight of the house mouse,
the cost of good meat, of transit for people who straddle three cities.
- Busting the cap off a beer with the table, I fail
to come in on the bridge, get lost like a tourist, embarrassed.

The cost of good meat, of transit for people who straddle three cities,
It's hard out here! – I know. It's hard to sing the blues and be happy. You
came in on the bridge, got lost like a tourist, an embarrassed
phone call from the Esso on Airport. We walked to your new place in the rain.

It's hard out here, I know. It's hard to sing the blues and be happy. Your
impact lures the mice out that live in the walls. You
call a cab to the Esso on Airport, we walk from your place in the rain
as the dusk blurs the boundaries of our bodies, our lines.

Your impact lures the mice out that live in the walls. You
get them moving, run your rhythm through the house.
As the dusk blurs the boundaries of our bodies, our lines,
we imagine ourselves unkillable. And free.

A Guide to THE ERASURE OF SPANDAU PRISON
(SEE ALSO: "1+1-1=1"; "the housing of Nazi war criminals"; "1-1")

First, a few short words about mass:
  It's that which is unchanging
  in an object. Even in absence
  of the object, it stays — in smaller
  pieces, solutions, new forms. Planets
  begat rock that begat buildings that brought nations, cities,

wars — then the insoluble and washing clean. Someone said,
And then it was good. But what defence against forgetting

can we limit ourselves for this?

    In 1987, they knocked down
    Spandau Prison, ground her oldness
    into dust and drowned her
    in the ocean. No one asked for anything else.

In the city where she stood: the lime
unsomething of a parking lot,
where thousands of citizens whittled into
an *objects minus history* haze burrow through
the buying of meats,
cheeses, bottled water.

The local stuff's too impure
for drinking, something about
minerals, too many parts
per millions.

A Guide to THE MATERIAL RECORD

(SEE ALSO: *"resurfacing"; "the decline of the Atlantic fishing fleet"; "decline"*)

Sheer and shore on the first cinnamon dawn of the year,
catch a blank stare off the Eskimo-ground and you
walk, no, goose-step, toes to the sky, towards one of our
four hundred nameless bays. Bring the dog with you.
Let him bound through the snow-crust like some giddy,
runaway, sine-wave. Indecipherable by his tracks.

You go belly down, serpentine, up to the praying drifts
who give space, solace to her forgotten shell.
The idol of our ocean, so damn old. So old
we can't remember or forget it, it's just there,
ubiquitous, like the tints of trees, the stars, the sky.

You get there ahead of me and chisel off a rotting,
embryonic flake, frosted beyond the word *metal*.
Yell out when it's done and I'll ready my mittens,

cover my face and get set to accept it – Arrow,
your dagger from the sky. Sharp, so sharp.

Sharp enough to dice the ocean, or bring your
autocratic step-dad to his knees. It bounces off my
well-vested chest and drops in two perfect pieces at my feet.
Gathered up, they're ours. Yin and yang, they're the
Best and *Friends* lockets, with an added story to tell.

The last, best, cargo of a forgotten ship's hull.
Two charms and the death-rattle of industry.

A Guide to GETTING IT WRONG

(SEE ALSO: *"an owner's guide to evolution"*; *"organic inks"*; *"Piltdown Men"*)

In the future,
we'll have animals
genetically improved upon
to do our daily tasks: birds to clean our houses,

dogs that drive cars. Anthropologists,
while unearthing the vault at
Hanna-Barbera, will convince their
benefactors
that the Flintstones were more advanced
than the Jetsons.

It will be recorded on their textkittens
and taught to kids by bats.

A Guide to THE DEATH OF DR. HAING S. NGOR

(SEE THE FILM: The Killing Fields (1984); "*martyrdom: case histories*", page 125)

First there was Cambodia, and what followed
that was hell. Then there was America,
which led to heaven. How's that sound

for spin? First there was a wife, kids, big
pagan women needing knives, syringes,
drips. Then there was a locket, an

extended young relation in a China-
town apartment. How's that for
expensive? First there was

a dedication to the arts, the coo of
Hollywood. Then there was Oliver Stone, days
and the catharsis of women who

would do anything

    once. Revulsion, rejection. A man

    talking to immigrants in a bus-station alley.

        First, there were beginnings. Then,

continuation. The tension in a quiet man's

    walk, something like middle age that's

        wet from the defrosting. First, there was

the *Tribune*, then the *Star*, then a special

    E.T. retrospective, your niece with flowers.

        Salute this. Your image at the Oscars, smiling

past the cellos. All that clapping, *ratta-*

    tat-tat. Ratta-tat. Woot. First, there was a howl,

        neighbours emptied in the square. A car with

a burnt body aborted to the seat. A child's skinned

    neckline. A wife: *Hysterical!* you said, *I am not*

        a doctor! A locket and the demand for

that locket. *De-wombing*, you used to
call it, *hysterectomies*. The sound of
one submission, *ratta-*

tat-tat. First there was Cambodia, then

America, then the whole idea
of irony bleeding
out on a one-way street.

A Guide to CONSCIENTIOUSNESS

(SEE ALSO: *"the pay gradient of gadflies"; "crow-meat recipes"; "smiling public men"*)

Here comes a word, so proud you can hear it
applauding in the back of your throat. As a kid I

dug up anthills with the whipper-snipper, not just
dug them up, but burrowed in neck-deep, blister-

buzzing, all violent automation chucking through
the undergrass. Dirt rained home and the lawn

reoriented around a new plane, decided on bottoms and tops.
I went on to win and to lose. I got older. Nations rearranged,

and now address each other differently. Cop-outs are
too simple for anything but metaphor. Simile, even

suggests that opinions are different, though they might
share a common root. There is room for

departure between them. But soft consensus hopes
they're the same mass creation, and with effort

everyone can be right and
warm within the bullshit of

A Company Word
like *conscience*. Give me
art that's decided, just

once. Give me someone who's
read everything and knows what

they like and don't like. Allow me time to
decide if I agree, a year or so in the cellar

where they keep the banned books, food and
water, some paper to write stuff down.

A Guide to GETTING IT RIGHT

(SEE ALSO: *"context and connotation"; "subtext riddles"; "fashion"; "taste"*)

Rescind your faith
in synonyms. They don't
exist. Understand
           that language is
like any living creature, a product
of forever-evolution.

And no one suggests that
               two animals

are the same thing, even when
someone does, they're just
waving at the species with
catch-all categories like
birds, dogs, or bipeds.

Know how to map out
the space a word makes, how no
part of it is something else at all.
    Put ten properties together
in a sentence, let your nation shape around
the holes you've left unfilled. I had this cat
        growing up that
got hit by a car, my mother said he
went away, then
passed on, and then
died.

Appendix A

VARIOUS WORLD:

THE PINSKY VARIATIONS

(Amour//Bounty//College//Drought//Encoded//Farting//Girls//Homily//
Inklings//Jazz//Kinship//Ledgers//Marx//Nightmares//Op-Ed//
Palliative//Queued//Rhythm//Saboteurs//Tokyo//Utero//Volunteers//
Weed//Exhibit//Yearling//Zeugma)

The Shape of the Box: AN INTRODEDICATION

Obviously, any dedication has to start with Robert Pinsky himself. His name is in the title, and he wrote the poem "ABC," which inspired this series. I don't know the man, but have always loved his work. In a perfect world, he would come across these someday and like them, I haven't asked for any sort of permission. There are rules, and these are they:

1. All poems must be twenty-six words long, with the first letters of each word spelling out our beloved, beleaguered Roman alphabet.

2. The only symbol used, apart from grammatical ones, is the equals sign (=), as this was used in the original poem. It's included in the first piece here as an homage.

3. The lone allowable deviation from the source is the inclusion of words that sound out the letter X phonetically (i.e., words that start with "ex-" or "es-"). Pinsky didn't allow himself any such alteration, though he also didn't write twenty-six of these things. I suppose he might have, and he just didn't publish them. He is a better writer than I am, so he may have stuck to just the letter and not the sound the letter makes.

As a further note, some have labelled Pinsky's poem an abecedarian. I am hesitant to do the same with these, as I prefer the stricter definition of that form, which is to say a variation on an acrostic where the first letter of each line in a twenty-six-line poem spells out the alphabet. It doesn't matter, in the end. I just wanted to say this before someone else did.

AMOUR

Alone, beauty can't deliver euphoria forever.

Good hearts, I justly keep longer.

Miscible natures outpace quaint romances.

Sometimes truth undercuts vanity.

When X's (*homage*➔) = your Zion.

BOUNTY (or, the BUD LITE of grapes)

After book-writing
comes dinner (enough for good health).

I juggle kindreds, liking my
nachos or pasta (quick repasts) served
to underscore value-priced wines.

Especially you, Zinfandel.

COLLEGE

Academic breaks can deflect encroaching frustrations (grades, heartbreak, intellectual jester-kings leering mocking noses over pupils' quarterly reports . . .)

Students take uniform vacations wetly,
expelling yeasty
zoomorphisms.

DROUGHT

A
browning
crop
dries ever further. Grey havens in July
keep livestock moistened,
nourished.

Once precipitation quits, rainmakers scratch through undersoil.

Vacated watermarks exhume yielded zombies.

ENCODED

Afft'h bfomlx Ct dirq ejlmvog fowfi gifowfi hiivtt. Ibmhnnve jvrfg kbitvt lqvo, mftbgjmh npwfio ojuf. Pjopdbguh qvnq ro, sjtiojtigjmh tsvfwz upol'h vuvsmbo wfufmdvmvthovth.

Xpmdovhjlo: Ybmhhhi zthvnqgjlo.

Note: The preceding poetic cipher is written in a real code with a real underlying pattern. If you can figure out the pattern and crack the poem, please email your solutions to "THE HIDDEN (m)EANING OF POETRY CONTEST" at jacob709_902@hotmail.com. All correct answers will be rewarded with a free bonus poem written by this book's creator. The poem will be at least thirty lines long and quality-checked by other poets, some of whom may have even won awards for their work.

FARTING

Able bodies can digest easy foods. Guts hunker in jumbled knots: liquefying meat, nourishing organs, packaging quaffed remains.

Stomachs twist untreatables violently,

wheezily expelling yowling zephyrs.

GIRLS

At boyhood, coveting debuts. Estrogen

(female growth hormone) insists juveniles keep

lasting mates. Now, often people quit relationships surreptitiously.

This underwrites vendettas, whose expenses yield zillions.

HOMILY

Anonymity before Christ Divine! extolled father.

(God has influenced judges, killed legions,
motivated numerous Olympians, parted
quaking Red Seas.)

*Thus, unpretentiousness, vicar wagers,
exalts your zenith.*

INKLINGS

Automated brushes can draw exact figures,
grasping *"how."*

Iconoclasts joke, keeping leaders modest,
neutralizing our politicians' quarrelsome
rhetoric. Subversive thinkers understand visuals.

"Why?"
extracts yuk-yuks, zingers.

JAZZ

After Blues
came Duke Ellington, fantasists granting
hot impressions.

Just keep listening, more notes open phrasing. Quietly.

Rebel syncopation triggered ultramodernism –
Virtuosos with ecstatic yo-yo zap!

KINSHIP

August beckons, coming down eager from
grey hiatus. In July, kites
languish meditatively, no one
pales. Quercus rejuvenates, summer's thick underbrush veils
worms, expands yeastlike, Zen-ward.

LEDGERS

– Accountants balance cheque books, divvy earnings.

– Financial gurus help influence judiciaries, knowingly laundering money.
Notice our pols quit reading scoops that
(*uncovered*)
villains wrote?

Expensive yardwork?
– Zillions . . . .

MARX (or, post-MARX)

As   bureaucracy

crumbles,   declining

empires fall –

galvanized hopefuls

incarcerate juntas, kidnapping

leaders. Mavericks negate occupied palaces. Quickly,

rebels solidify, tighten up.

Vigilante warriors extol

young zealots.

NIGHTMARES

At bedtime, child-dreamers envision falcons, gorillas, hyenas.

Illusions jar kids, leaving
mental operations paralyzed, quaking.

Revellers suffer through
unconscious visions, which exacerbate youthful zoophobia.

OP-ED

Any bonehead can draft editorials. Fact gets hidden in jurist-kept lies.

Mannered neanderthals openly persecute qualified rebuttals. Somehow, these unassailable, vile weasels express your zoanthropy.

PALLIATIVE

All big cities
display environmental failures.

Gaseous harbingers
invade jungles, killing less
malevolent occupiers. Parents quickly
react, saving trees, unlearning violences, while

expecting Your Zion.

QUEUED

Alcoholics beg change, drivers exchange furrowed glances. Hastily, I jump knotted lines, make noise on phone, quaff Rolaids (stomach threatening ulceration).

Vacantly worshipping Xmas?

Yes, zealously.

RHYTHM

A beat can drive

       energy forward. Giving hooks

insistent jingles keeps listeners

motivated. Notice older pianists

       quietly reading signage; technical understanding

varies Wagner, expands yammering zydeco.

SABOTEURS

Ants become cannibals during elongated famine. Greedily, hungry
individuals justify killings, leaving
                                 military openings. Predators quickly react,

striking
through un-
                    apologetically

(. . . victims writhe, exhausted)   (. . . yellowing ziggurat).

TOKYO

Aliens battle
carnivorous dinos. Easterners faint, get hunted.

Individuals juke killers, leaving mutants (NUCLEAR
OPPRESSION!) P-O'ed. Quakes rattle seaside towns, unleashing
voracious water.
Excitement yields zeitgeist.

UTERO

Angst
begets cadence, depression exhausts. Friends go home

inseparable.

Jokes keep levity, make normalcy. Other (petty) quagmires

resolve,

so tension understands velocity.

Who's expecting? Your zygote?

VOLUNTEERS

As barometers climb, drought endangers forests. Good higher-ups insist judiciously kitted leaders manage operations, patrolling quandongs, redwoods.

Skipping that, unprotected vegetation would experience years zeroed.

WEED

Amateur botanists can derive euphoria from grassy harvests. In joint-knowledgeable lands, marijuana not only provides quiet relaxation, smokers toke uninhibited. Vilifying wakefulness extends yesterday's zealotries.

EXHIBIT

Art: Because calamity drives ever forward.

Ghosts: Hung innovators.

Juries: Kahlo's lips, mapping "No," or "Please."

Quiet: Rabid silence.

Tragedy: Unfinished variations, with expectant, youthful zeal.

YEARLING

A bear cub died
early, frost gathered him
in January. Kneeling, local men
noticed owl pelts, quills reddened.

Sacrificing
those unconnected –   Vengeance,
                           we're exporting you (*Zoonosis*).

ZEUGMA

A boy couldn't draw, even faces. God help it, Jake (*know-it-all!*), liking music, now offers poetry. Quiet! Resolved study!

Targets: Unearthed vocabulary! Written exercise!

: Yen!   Zlotys!

Appendix B

CONTRAST NEGOTIATIONS, '05–'07

Hardly revolutionary. One single certainty caught in the infinity sign of the swerve. Donna and me got blasted at the riverside, rolled up into her Rabbit like cannons with gunpowder freckles. We didn't know any better, or we did but hadn't learned it all too well. Fifteen or eighteen or one years old.

The Oldenburg Hotel required fresh paint on the dividing line, they liked to look good from the road. The highway had different names depending where you came from. I came from the ocean but my parents were Interiors. The road thought that things changed as you began to move around them, I say this and hope you don't assume I disagreed.

Donna stuck her top half out the driver's side window. I pushed against mine for balance. She snaked her front left tire in and out of the new yellow, all the while shouting half slogans with the butt of her voice. *Getyerassesoutta* – pauses to twist the tires, *Comeonwakethefuck* – tightens her fishtail noose around the middle. We ran the full kilometre of four-hour-old updates and I only stared at her ass pushed up against the headrest once. The fresh paint ran out at Marriott's Cove. We didn't notice, kept the pattern of our Rothko brush ramming through the coast until arrival, whiplashed, in my driveway.

She sat back in her seat and measured me through the rearview intermediary. She said *Happy Birthday*. Fifteenth or eighteenth or first. She told me to get out, put her hand to her face as I left. Hardly revolutionary; one single certainty stuck in the infinite. Like the promise of collision lined up against the breakneck exhumations of the night.

The Difference Between
THE FILM *PSYCHO* (1960) AND MY SISTER, FIVE YEARS YOUNGER

Nothing. Nothing and nothing and nothing, then burnt. My skin holds out past April, only to smear up like blood on a fictional porcelain, all mysteries archived by the Queen's weekend. A tan waits around like the Blue Jays' season chances, a really bad road trip and we're dead.

Now it hurts to look happy, also to say *ironic*. I can't see how we share all these genes and you end up by August looking like a perfectly ripe banana fried in gold – your red hair sheltering bronze deposits on your shoulders, like an infant from some species of cat that carry their young on their back.

Your freckles bind together like dew overnighting on a park bench. When you wouldn't stop crying I'd splash water on your face. Dad came downstairs and I told him Mom did it.

The Difference Between
MY SISTER AND OLIVER SACKS'S BOOK *AWAKENINGS*

The seeing isn't spiritual. The seeing is literal. It has little to do with the sea, for example.

Cait went two years pretending she didn't need glasses. She sat in every front row, buttressing her head forward in her hands like the Sphinx squinting in a sandstorm. She walked headlong into light poles, guessed wrong on the stairs and left a tooth in the carpet. She ate three bites of a cat food and cucumber sandwich, I knew and didn't tell her. Once, she scolded the ottoman. The myopic are gifted at metaphor.

You could say that the blind were born for mornings. One can short out brain cells by waking up to the sun. The attention is bad, too, for the sun's enigmatic reputation, the secrets of the eight-minute laser-train to Earth. Cait came home from the doctor's, took one look at my mother's harsh rosacea, and went out to a different doctor for a list of prescription muds. That was the summer she quit baseball and took up watching tv in the den.

There are plants that excel under diffused light, that do best in greenhouses or sheltered by walls. But how did they come to be like this in nature? I wonder if these plants mistake the same things we do, like if they ever say *open* when they really mean *on*. For the first three weeks, Cait kept asking to switch her lenses with me. We'd fall about the living room, drunk on the rewiring, dizzy from refraction. The way she hides her face from the sunlight makes me think she was there for the initial burst and followed it down, like she's forever eight minutes too old for this world. I, too, would be embarrassed. I would keep my eye line low.

The Difference Between
ST. VALENTINE AND THE 1994 OLYMPIC HOCKEY SCHEDULE

Paul Kariya. Peter Nedved. That kid we had in net. I remember February and the old TV in my parents' room that shuffled its deck when the wind gusted up. A box of candy hearts my mom gave me. The white duvet. I remember the white duvet and the little red hearts, lined up on the duvet like buttons. I remember Mom complaining when she found them in the covers. I was told to make them last. Budgets and limits and goals.

I decided to eat one to start every period, one for each big save, big hit, big play. This was the winter they closed the fishery and all the rich kids' mailboxes got clubbed into the street. I remember the sound of the wind through the chimney, *this is how they live in Norway.* I remember the news was on when I called down, *We beat the Italians, We scored short-handed, It's 3–1.* I remember being reminded that the news was on. I remember being reprimanded. I remember Paul Kariya, the announcer was in love with him in secret. We laughed about this in school *because faggots were funny back then.*

I remember that Finland came third, formal dress at the finals. I remember the boys discussing who'd take the shots in overtime. I remember Nedved scoring: gulp a heart. I remember

Kariya missing: one aside. I remember Forsberg slipping one under the kid's white glove to end it. I remember the Swedes had more fans there than we did. I remember Paul Kariya. He was crying on the bench. If I was crying, no one told me.

The Difference Between
THE STICKER PRICE AND MY (SELF-SERVING) VIEW OF SUCCESS

There's no hope for casus belli with children born like this, their lives are a series of pre-tests, of overtures. And Ami drove the Mustang like the background of a clothing ad, even at ten past the sign she seemed somehow slow-motioned. Her friends pre-tanned for what the Almanac claimed was coming, my flushed red head stood out in proportion like a novelty balloon doll propped up in the passenger's seat.

Ami came from boarding school in Maine, came from aristocratic Democrats, came with five big bags to go driving, all one hundred pounds of her squished inward by the weight. I once saw a pop can like that in science class, needed a vacuum to remind it it was empty. She came two days early and slept off a bender, came prepared with matches, came hard in the back of her boyfriend's nuzzle car, her eyes sixteen-years-wide with revelation like maybe that feeling was the cliché falling out of her.

Beautiful girls understand their sports cars,

better than some dumpy mechanic. They know why people buy silk car-covers, they sleep in plain sight of their mirrors. Her friends rode in back, six feet stuck through the space between our seats like half a dozen stems in a bucket, painted red. Proximity left me with hope for promotion, hope of being shrugged forward by any of the million tiny Atlases that make up an Ami's vista. Ami glanced regally at the farm families' mailboxes, at their clawed-fingered barn roofs, each gesturing hopefully at their tiny plot of skyline, where she might fix her opal eyes, and nod.

And there was the smell of menthols, of the DMV's fresh laminate. And the light smell of comfort, forever circling around itself, with custom rims and the price tag left on.

The Difference Between
KING KONG ARRIVES IN EDO (1936) AND THE CAFÉ WHERE HE FELL

Some sonic thump and then a fissure in the sidewalk that straddled off thirty feet to martyr on the beach. *Know me.* Compressed air (like diamonds), or towed warboats, or dust – Whatever, it pushed harder against this reclaimed city than the home front handicrafts holding her allowed.

Gojira, now there was a collectivist cultural hero – all melted metal, no divisions or schisms where a ghost might grow (and develop a female fan base, and become a magnet for creationists' bad jokes, and experience love, induced seizures from a thousand bee stings, vertigo, death, renewal at nine-thirty, three shows a day/six on Sundays).

No one who made the movie is alive any more. Nobody who watched it has all that much to say. The producers invested in levels of light, five pizza-shaped cartons in a flatbed on the highway. In the movie, you don't see what happens to the hero, he just fades from history and we have to guess they burned him. All future viewings are projected in memory. When the last print bombed out, the wake was called off.

The only proof we have that he was here is this slice through the street outside the new American coffeehouse. An old man with no teeth holds up a creased photograph. In the background, between the decade-flakes and his smudge of younger face, is a poster. Star-shaped, the woman screams in a voice so high-pitched, we can't hear it, though it tore the corner from the sheet. This man says he saw her: *This is what the monster wanted. He touched her here and I laughed.*

The Difference Between
MISSISSAUGA AND THE MAN ON THE MOON

You can tell it's Ontario by the squares. The farmer-tanned land plots through the bunkered creek like a fleet of sacrificial pawns approaching the lake's impervious defences. Score one for the ungeometric resistance.

The airplane banks and shifts like a motorcross on a coastal backroad. I shut my plastic cover to the drama below me and focus on the general's tent version mapping by on digital display. It's best to remain emotionally distant. That's why I love flying and know nothing about how it works: magic, moxie, the wind? Like any miracle, flight begins by shoving a wedge between the world and what keeps it all together.

Concentric suburbia spins out like citronella spirals from a central starting point – Urbia? The Trans-Can's exit strategies scribble S's and O's through the owner's compensated cornfields. Way to take one for the team,

civilian. We can read that message you're spelling out from here.

The Difference Between
ENGLISH STANDARDS AND THE ANGLES OF AN ISOSCELES TRIANGLE

Plus I used to know this teacher, we'll call him Mr. Bluejeans. Mr. Bluejeans went to great lengths to hide his French accent. You could say that my district was somewhat closeted and it was best to blend in when entrusted with the future of the plastics factory workforce. I only bring it up because Mr. Bluejeans taught me French. This might be why I never get past *Salut* with store clerks in Quebec before having them grimace back to English.

I don't want you to think that I'm ragging on poor Mr. Bluejeans, this isn't about what you might think it's about. *Start over.* The thing is in parts of Newfoundland, teachers still lock kids in at recess for adding S's to the ends of verbs. Whatever, it can't be easy to teach away the world. I didn't go to grade school there, but I spent three years adding range to my *oranges*, yellowing out my *yeyyous* (adding lines to lean my yeahs against). Here's another irony: they kept me out of art class to do it.

I'm not saying there's anything wrong with precision. I'm just mad I never learned to paint. My problem is I always draw the outlines too heavy, then as I fill it in I realize, say, that there's more apple there than that. No, I'm lying.

I've never painted more than a monochromatic shingle, though when I'm bored sometimes in class, I'll doodle out connected triangles, each addition sharing one of the same lines as the last, and maybe inside one of those triangles, there's a small French man painting apples, wondering how he can push past the tight corners to make his *sujet* look fuller, more round than the wall would procedurally allow.

The Difference Between
QC 980 (METEOROLOGY) AND QC 995 (THE WEATHER)

From a certain height, you can sense the geopolitics of storms. Separate schools of raindrops push against each other, and in the pushing, disappear. A cross section of the chaos reflects down my windowpane. All learning is like this. There are birds that can inform us on the quantity of mammals, there are rocks that warn about earthquakes.

Came here thinking I'd be back in half an hour. Didn't work out that way. Didn't bring my wallet, walked. Bus pass smiles back at me from home. I hold off a yawn as it strikes me as redundant to yawn in a library, sort of like coughing in a morgue.

Behind me, every inch of understanding is bound together in the concrete. Books are a dismissal of the unity of everything, our ability to hold it in our hands, or be held. Four stories from my reference point, umbrellas with pants pound into the rain. The boneless interaction. The wind that you can see.

It takes the whole morning, but eventually the sun melts away the clouds like a hatching Polaroid. At once, all three million volumes turn their faces to her rays. It causes a deep vibration. In the basement, the foundation cracks, you can hear the groan for days.

Postscripture

Thank you to: all extensions of my family and especially my dad, the folks at MUN (Susan, Mary, etc.), my teachers and fellow students at the Guelph MFA, my enablers at M&S (Anita, Ellen, Molly, etc.), and all the losers I've been known to hang out with. Specific gratuity is directed to the following early readers: Mike in Halifax, Stephen in St. John's, Dave B., Bill D., John S., and Matt DiG. in GAMErica.

Certain previsions of these poems were unleashed on the following markets: The Laura Hird Showcase (virtual), the *Literary Review of Canada* (real), Mannequin Envy (real, and virtual), My Favorite Bullet (virtual), Nthposition (virtual), *Prairie Fire* (real), Remark (real), and Zygote In My Coffee (virtual, then real).

The Lester Bangs epigraph is from the essay "The Incredibly Strange Creatures Who Stopped Living and Became Mixed-Up Zombies, or, The Day the Airwaves Erupted," originally published in the March 1973 issue of *Creem* magazine and reprinted in his posthumous collection *Psychotic Reactions and Carburetor Dung*, edited by Greil Marcus. Published by Anchor Books.

The excerpt that precedes "A Guide to Syncopation" is from Don McKay's "Bone Poems," taken from *Camber: Selected Poems* by Don McKay © 2004. Published by McClelland & Stewart Ltd. Used with permission of the publisher.

"A Guide to Alternate Histories" contains lyrics from the song "Basket Case" by U.S. pop-punk band Green Day. The song is from their 1994 album *Dookie*.

"A Guide to the House at 6 Arthur Hatt Road" is dedicated (with the only absolute truths that I know) to my mother, Janet Mooney.

The italicized passage "objects minus history" in "A Guide to the Erasure of Spandau Prison" is derived from the expression "objects without history," first coined by the scholar Edward Said when talking about deconstruction in colonial historiography. Being an "object without history" is a very bad thing, I think it could quite possibly be the worse thing there is.

The appendix *Various World: The Pinsky Variations* is inspired by and dedicated to Mr. Robert Pinsky, whom I've never met but who wrote the poem "ABC" that gave the sequence both its inspiration and its name. The poem "Op-Ed" in said section is lovingly dedicated to the staff and readership of the *Toronto Sun*.

If any discrepancies appear between the version of events reported herein and reality, the latter shall prevail. But if it wasn't what happened, it can still be what happens. The collection as a whole is dedicated to the memory of *Kirby Puckett* and to the good people at the *Wikimedia Foundation*. Until next time, folks, take care of yourselves. And each other.